PIONEER SETTLERS OF NEW FRANCE

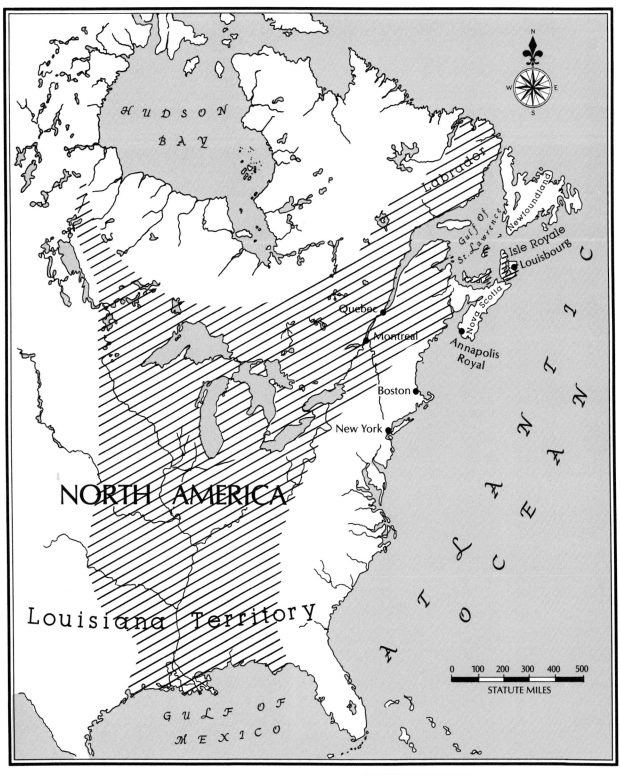

HUDSON
BAY

Labrador

Gulf of
St. Lawrence

Newfoundland

Isle Royale
Louisbourg

Quebec

Montreal

Nova Scotia

Annapolis
Royal

Boston

New York

NORTH AMERICA

Louisiana Territory

ATLANTIC OCEAN

GULF OF
MEXICO

0   100   200   300   400   500
STATUTE MILES

Shaded areas represent French
holdings in North America in 1744.

Pioneer Settlers of New France

by Joan Anderson
photographs by George Ancona

LODESTAR BOOKS
Dutton   New York

Other books by Joan Anderson with photographs by George Ancona

Spanish Pioneers of the Southwest

Christmas on the Prairie

The First Thanksgiving Feast

From Map to Museum

The Glorious Fourth at Prairietown

Joshua's Westward Journal

Pioneer Children of Appalachia

A Williamsburg Household

Library of Congress Cataloging-in-Publication Data

Anderson, Joan.
 Pioneer settlers of New France / by Joan Anderson; photographs by
George Ancona.—1st ed.
  p. cm.
  "Lodestar books."
  Summary: Text and photographs recreate eighteenth-century life in a pioneer settlement in Nova Scotia.
  ISBN 0-525-67291-5
  1. Canada—History—To 1763 (New France)—Juvenile literature.
 2. Frontier and pioneer life—Canada—Juvenile literature.
 3. Pioneers—Canada—History—Juvenile literature. [1. Frontier and pioneer life—Canada. 2. Canada—History—To 1763 (New France)]
 I. Ancona, George, ill. II. Title.
F1030.A46 1990   89-34991
971.01—dc20   CIP
                            35476   AC

Published in the United States by Lodestar Books, an affiliate of Dutton Children's Books, a division of Penguin Books USA Inc.

Published simultaneously in Canada by Fitzhenry & Whiteside Limited, Toronto

Editor: Rosemary Brosnan   Designer: Marilyn Granald, LMD

Printed in the U.S.A.   First Edition

10 9 8 7 6 5 4 3 2 1

to Dan Masterson
J.A.

to Beverly Reingold
G.A.

Introduction

Imagine what North America must have looked like two hundred and fifty years ago! To Europeans, it was a vast, virgin continent bursting with surprises and riches. As a result, the great powers of the time—France, England, and Spain—all wanted possession of it.

Our story focuses on the French, whose explorers had claimed territory extending from northern Canada down through the Great Lakes, south along the Mississippi River, and ending in Louisiana. French fur trappers and fishermen settled in these territories, anxious to turn a profit by selling the natural resources of this untapped region.

Gradually it became clear that the French territory in what is now Canada, particularly Nova Scotia, was more valuable than anyone had ever expected because of the fertile fishing banks that surrounded this easternmost portion of North America. This was a period in history when many of the people in Europe were Roman Catholic and the Church declared 135 fasting days per year. This meant that Catholics were permitted to eat only fish on these days. With such a demand for fish, the waters around Europe were being depleted and fish would have to be imported from far away. As a result, adventuresome French merchants and fishermen scurried off to New France in order to reap the benefits of this demand.

Our story is set in Louisbourg, the grandiose fortress town that welcomed not only the new workers but also ships from all over the world. The fortress had been constructed in 1713, at first to protect the French capital, Quebec City, and Montreal. But it was soon populated with soldiers and sailors sent to maintain and defend this vital fishing area. Built on a grand scale and looking very much like a great castle that belonged in Europe, it hardly seemed to be penetrable. And yet, because of unreliable weather patterns and a short growing season, almost all necessities—food, drink, clothing, building supplies—had to be imported. Louisbourg could only survive and maintain its continental way of life if it kept in contact with the rest of the world.

As a result, when France declared war on England in 1744, the very dependent Louisbourg began to crumble. Trade with the New England colonies halted and shipping lanes between New France and Europe closed down.

The demise of the French holdings will be seen through the eyes of two boys—Jean François Lelarge, whose uncle owns a fleet of merchant ships, and Pierre André, whose father manages a fleet of fishing boats.

Up until the summer of 1744 their lives have been filled with the promise of opportunity and their professional futures seemed assured. But, as the French fortunes decline, they will be forced to scatter and relocate, taking only their survival instincts, garnered from settlement life, and their heritage with them.

Pierre André watched his father disappear down the foggy path that led to the garrison town of Louisbourg, and hoped that he would bring back sorely needed supplies. His stomach growled at the thought of having meat and fruit, which he had not tasted for months now.

It was a cold, dreary day in May, usually the month when shipping lanes would reopen from Europe and the West Indies, and the seaport would be bustling with sailors and all the provisions that came with them.

But so far not one ship had graced the harbor since last November! It depressed Pierre to peer out at the lonely bay. He couldn't help but wonder if France had actually gone to war, as was rumored. It was frustrating to be cut off from the rest of the world. For the first time in his sixteen years, he was frightened for the very survival of this settlement, which was dependent on Europe for almost all of its food, clothing, and provisions.

At least the gulls are satisfied, Pierre mused, as he watched a flock of gray and white scavengers land on the beach outside his window and gobble up scraps of fish left over from yesterday's catch. Too bad *we* can't survive on scraps, he thought, and went back to balancing the André account books.

Just then he heard the morning drumroll and assumed that his father would be approaching the town gate.

"Who goes there?" a lone guard called out, straining to see the figure emerging from the fog.

"Can't you smell the fish?" Pierre's father answered, joking with the guard as he strode across the drawbridge.

"Ah, it is only you, Monsieur André," the young soldier exclaimed, relaxing his military stance and motioning him onward.

Security was very tight in Louisbourg because the French settlers had much to protect. Not only was their harbor one of the busiest in the New World, but Nova Scotia was surrounded by some of the richest fishing banks in the world.

Monsieur André and many other Frenchmen had left their homeland some twenty years ago for a more prosperous life in New France. The fishing industry ensured large profits in exchange for hard work, and a chance to elevate their station in society. Up until now the New World had not disappointed Monsieur André and his family, and he hoped his good fortune was not about to change.

This place is magnificent! Monsieur André thought, pausing to take a whiff of the brisk salt air before proceeding on. He picked his way through all of the people and carts and bales that cluttered Rue Toulouse, and relished the activity, which was such a contrast to the tranquil setting of the fishermen's houses.

Despite the tensions that existed because of the threat of war, there was an air of permanence and security that came from living in a garrison town. But today he was saddened each time he gazed out at the empty harbor.

A sudden burst of cannon fire pierced the air, shaking Monsieur André back to reality. The cannon was being fired quite regularly these days to direct ships, lost in the fog, toward the safety of the harbor.

Eventually he came to the Lelarge Magasin and bounded up the steps of the store, finding the rotund merchant and his earnest young nephew, Jean François, huddled over a pile of recent orders.

"Ah, *bonjour, bonjour,*" the affable Lelarge said, extending his hand in greeting.

"*Bonjour,*" the fisherman answered, nodding in Jean's direction. "So, I see your uncle has you working hard as usual, my boy. I left Pierre doing the same thing," he continued. " 'Tis good we have young men eager to apprentice in our businesses, eh, Lelarge?"

The merchant heartily agreed while Jean only smiled weakly. He barely tolerated storehouse work, preferring life around the waterfront. Perhaps he felt that way because his French ancestors had all been fishermen. Orphaned five years ago, Jean was sent to live with Uncle Claude in hopes that opportunities in New France would assure his future.

"So what can I do for you today?" Lelarge inquired halfheartedly, knowing his boxes and barrels were pathetically barren.

"I should be most grateful to have *any* staples," Monsieur André answered. "My fishermen are refusing to work unless I give them better food and clothes. They say they risk their lives at sea these days."

"Undoubtedly true," the merchant answered. "Things are getting treacherous. Two of my best ships, the *Argonaut* and the *Suzannah,* are overdue. I fear they've encountered trouble with those Boston English."

"I wouldn't be surprised," Monsieur André replied. "My men saw a vessel overtaken not fifty leagues from this port."

"You don't say!" Lelarge gasped. "Sounds like there could be some truth to those predictions of war after all, aye?"

Jean had long since put down his pen and was listening intently to the two men whose conversation was mere speculation. He felt that he could add something other than conjecture about the alarming circumstances that were beginning to surface.

"Uncle Claude," he blurted out, anxious now to get involved in the subject at hand. "I think I could shed some light on the delayed vessels."

The two men turned toward Jean, having almost forgotten his presence. "You what?" Uncle Claude asked.

"If you would be so kind as to permit me to take leave, sir, perhaps by studying my maps and charts I could second-guess your captains."

"How's that, my boy?"

"Well, after three years of studying navigation, sir, it would be a real privilege, to say nothing of a challenge, to put my knowledge to practical use."

"Hmmm," Uncle Claude uttered, intrigued by the idea. "With little or no business here, my boy, I would be a fool to say no. Just make certain you bring me back some good news."

Jean François buried himself in a maze of nautical paraphernalia—maps, charts, tide tables, compasses, dividers— rerouting the *Suzannah,* which was coming from the West Indies. Jean felt powerful as he charted distances and calculated nautical miles. He took pride in having a skill that eluded others.

Studying maps reminded Jean of the sea voyage that had brought him to Louisbourg five years ago. The journey had left an indelible mark on the young man. He was drawn to the sea and anything connected to it, and dreamed of someday visiting exotic ports.

Periodically his aunt would stop by to check on his progress. She had heard the rumblings about war and knew, as the wife of a merchant, that problems were ahead as long as the harbor remained barren.

"Well, my dear," she asked pointedly on her fifth visit to Jean's attic study, "surely you're making sense of the *Suzannah*'s delay, *oui*?"

"Indeed I am," Jean answered eagerly, rising to greet her. "I've come up with a few things. I should think Captain Decarrete could be encountering drifting icebergs as well as spring squalls. Surely he would have to sail with extreme caution to avoid trouble," Jean continued. "And furthermore, he would have to sail far away from the Boston harbor and those English waters if indeed we are at war. Having to take such precautions, I should think his voyage could easily be delayed a week or more."

Jean's conclusions were plausible enough to calm Uncle Claude's anxiety for a few days. Nevertheless, the underlying tension throughout the little fortress town was as thick as the walls that surrounded it.

Since there was very little work to do, each day seemed as long as a week and all eyes remained focused on the harbor. Jean noticed that his aunt and cousins were working diligently in the family garden, trying harder than usual to produce a good crop of vegetables. Perhaps they sensed the severity of the situation—that the garden was no longer merely a provider of condiments, but could become their sole source of food.

Fortunately, Uncle Claude had kept a few barrels of foodstuff for the family's consumption, and so far there wasn't a noticeable change in the quality of their meals.

One morning, about a week after making his predictions, Jean was preparing for another tedious day of warehouse work when he heard voices in the street below that sounded more jovial than troublesome. Looking out the window, he saw a man running toward the harbor wall. "A ship!" the man screamed. "Ship ahoy! Out yonder, by the point!"

Jean reached for his telescope and aimed it toward the harbor. His hand was shaking as he attempted to bring the vessel into focus. Sure enough, through the lens he could see a square-rigged ship rounding the point. She looked to be the size of the *Suzannah*. Still, Jean couldn't be certain that it was his uncle's ship until he recognized the figurehead. The wooden lady perched atop *Suzannah*'s bow was unmistakable.

His heart beat heavily as he watched the vessel glide closer to shore. It seemed like an eternity before the ship finally reached the harbor.

But a few minutes later his eyes feasted on the gilded lady with the red hair and turquoise gown, and Jean knew for sure. The *Suzannah* had come home!

"Uncle Claude," he shrieked, tearing from the house and running out onto the street. "Uncle!" he continued almost hysterically, entirely forgetting the decorum of a gentleman, which is always to remain calm and civilized. "The *Suzannah!*" he exclaimed. He ran swiftly, jumping over coils of rope and the barrels that cluttered the main street, and burst through the *magasin's* double doors. Huffing and puffing, he gestured toward the harbor, trying to explain to his uncle, between gasps of breath, what he had seen.

"Are you certain?" Uncle Claude countered.

"Believe me," answered Jean, exasperated that his uncle would even question him. "She should be dropping her sails any minute. Come, see for yourself."

The elder Lelarge grabbed his cane and the two headed for the wharf. A crowd had already gathered as was customary whenever there was an arrival in port. Several other merchants smiled bravely in Lelarge's direction, wishing it had been one of their vessels.

"Well, my boy," Uncle Claude said to his nephew, "you predicted she would arrive within the week and she did. Tomorrow you'll take the cargo lists and begin unloading. I think we're finally in business again."

While all of Louisbourg retreated that night inside their cozy, candlelit cottages, feeling safe and secure as the nightwatch made its hourly rounds in the cobblestone streets, Monsieur Lelarge conferred with the *Suzannah*'s captain and learned how dangerous the world outside had become.

"France has declared war on Great Britain, and sea battles have been raging furiously in Europe," he said. "It's only a matter of time," Captain Decarrete continued, "before Louisbourg and the other French colonies are affected. Once the hostilities begin in earnest, I believe that privateer raids will become a matter of course. It is my suggestion that you begin immediately to outfit your ships."

Lelarge could guess what was ahead. There would be no trading now with the New Englanders, which meant that Louisbourg would be without lumber and ample fresh food. Routine arrival of merchant ships from Europe and the West Indies would become uncertain. And outfitting his ships would surely be expensive. The excitement that came with *Suzannah*'s arrival quickly paled with the news that she delivered.

While his uncle met with Captain Decarrete, Jean scurried off to a cabaret usually frequented by the *Suzannah's* crew. Everything inside this dark and steamy world fascinated Jean. Scruffy sailors babbling in foreign tongues spoke of daring duels and ferocious storms. Sometimes they would break into songs so contagious that others would lift their mugs and join in.

But such revelry was starkly absent from the cabaret tonight. Some sailors, far gone from the effects of rum, sat silent, staring vacantly. Others eyed the barmaids as they sashayed among the tables but did little to attract their attentions. Jean detected an uncharacteristic weariness in the men. Among themselves, they talked of the possibility of not venturing out again unless their ships were properly outfitted with swivel guns and ammunition.

Jean ordered a second rum and tried to engage those next to him in conversation, but it soon became clear they wanted to lose themselves in simple board games and forget the voyage that was now behind them.

It was also a more somber uncle with whom Jean spoke the next day before heading off to the wharf.

"Remember, Jean," Uncle Claude cautioned, "never allow the cargo out of sight of the guards. This isn't just any shipment, you know. The whole town wants what we have and when your back is turned, who knows what might disappear."

"Very well," Jean said, trying to assure him but anxious to be off to tackle the job in his own way.

A tension hovered around the waterfront like a dense fog that showed no sign of lifting. The extra contingent of soldiers further contributed to the settlers' anxiety.

The job was monotonous as the shallop sailed or was rowed back and forth from ship to shore, bringing bales and barrels that were then hauled up onto the dock. Jean carefully checked each item off the cargo list, saw that it was loaded upon a cart, and followed each load up the street until it was safely hoisted into the attic of the storehouse.

One day, Jean spotted his friend Pierre hauling a pile of dried fish to market.

"*Bonjour!*" he called out.

"Ah, *bonjour,*" Pierre replied, always happy to be distracted from the job at hand. He instructed the servants to continue on with the delivery and stopped to chat with Jean. "So this is what you do when your uncle lets you out of the storehouse! How about selling us a bit of rum and meat right off the dock?"

"I can't do that," Jean answered, "but my uncle says that the fishermen will have their orders filled first."

"Well that's good news," Pierre answered, "as almost all our shore workers and fishermen are refusing to work unless we supply them with new rations."

"Things seem grim everywhere, Pierre," Jean said. "What do you think of the war?"

"I suppose it will make fishing at the Grand Banks a bit more dangerous, but I can't say I'll mind fending off those New Englanders, should I have to. It might just make my days out there, drifting about, more exciting."

Jean shook his head, amazed at Pierre's lackadaisical attitude, and wished he were more of a free spirit.

"I'll be interested to see how you'll be getting involved in the war effort," Pierre remarked as he turned to head back toward town. "They say we'll all have to take up military drill."

And with that he was gone, leaving Jean to ponder some sobering thoughts.

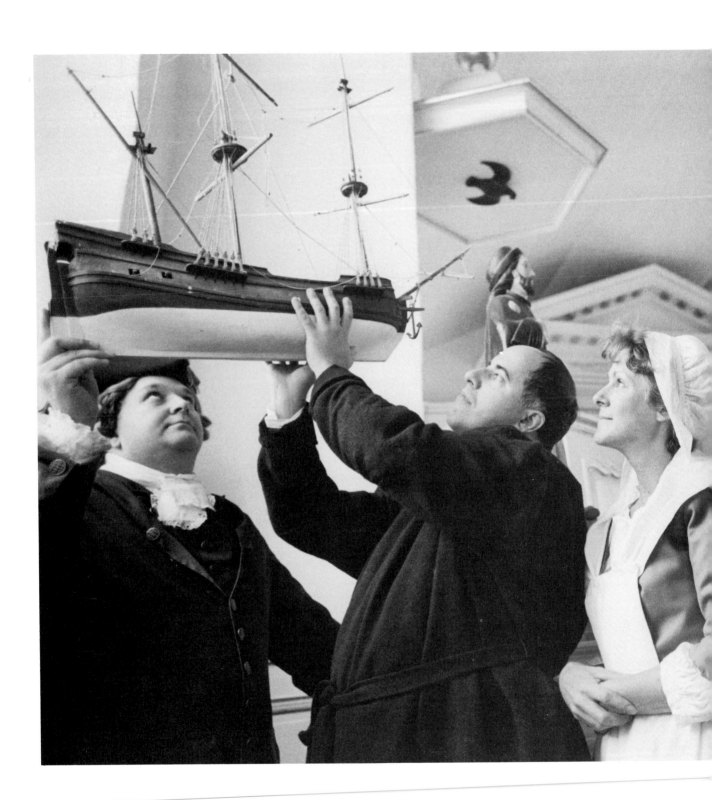

Obviously Uncle Claude had been contemplating a certain turn of events for weeks, as was evident when he came to collect his nephew after work one day.

"Jean, my boy, we shall be attending a special Mass today," Uncle Claude informed him. Jean was puzzled. Today wasn't Sunday or a saint's day. And his uncle was not very pious.

"I've concluded," Uncle Claude continued, "that God will not grant us any more favors unless we show Him our gratitude for His blessings of late."

"Indeed, sir," Jean said, still puzzled by his uncle's train of thought.

"And so several weeks ago I commissioned a craftsman to construct a ship model which looks very much like the *Suzannah*. We shall hang it in the church as a thankful gesture for her safe arrival. It is my thinking that by doing so we may be granted a similar favor in the safe arrival of the *Argonaut*."

Jean shook his head in amazement at his uncle's cunning, but nonetheless felt that taking a spiritual path in this crisis was probably wise. As the family gathered in the chapel, Jean prayed hard that this gesture would not be in vain.

The next few days were spent filling orders. While a steady stream of customers filed into the *magasin* from morning till night, Jean was sent off to inform the fishing proprietors to come collect their goods. "We must take care of those who feed us," Uncle Claude said time and time again. "It's the fish that make this place important. So we'd best keep the fishermen happy."

As he approached the village, Jean could see Pierre mending a string of fishnets and looking quite disgruntled.

"So, this is what you do when you're not out catching cod, aye?" Jean said, joking as Pierre had done with him several days before.

"It's not so funny," Pierre answered. "I've been doing all the common chores lately. My father thinks I'm one of his shore workers."

"Do they still refuse to work?" Jean asked.

"All but a few." He pointed to a small group preparing to clean today's catch. "I'm obliged to help them when I'm finished here."

"Well, the hard labor should be over for you soon, my friend. My uncle sent me here to tell your father that your order is ready. I think he even has boots and gloves, which should satisfy your fishermen for a while."

"With such news, I should think my father might be persuaded to give me the afternoon off. Want to join me for a sail?"

With the prospect of a break from his grueling schedule, Pierre plunged into the cleaning tasks with extra fervor. The table was overflowing with codfish, and he wasted no time grabbing their tails and chopping off the heads, making sure to remove the tongue and cheeks, which were a delicacy and brought in extra money. Quickly, he slit the bodies and laid them in the salting shed, where he sprinkled them with salt, and then breathed a sigh of relief.

With the grimy chores accomplished, he threw his apron aside, donned his warm jacket, and headed off.

Meanwhile, Jean had readied the shallop and was waiting on the beach. "This craft is too big for just the two of us," Pierre said as he approached his friend. They looked around for additional crew and found two shore workers eager to escape as well. Without further delay, they shoved off.

The shallop was headed straight for Petit Point, but their direction could change at the whim of the wind. Perhaps that's what Jean liked most about sailing—being at the mercy of the elements, working with the currents and wind directions, always taking your cue from nature. You couldn't be in a hurry and sail—there were too many variables that came into play. And best of all, once you set sail, no one could reach you until you were back on shore.

As they cut through the waters, with small waves splashing over the sides and into the boat, Jean all but forgot the problems that had been plaguing him and his uncle and the rest of the citizens of Louisbourg. Pierre held tight to the rudder and smiled at his friend as they sped along. The wind blew so strongly now that they didn't bother to speak to each other, since it was impossible to hear anything but the flapping of canvas and the roaring wind.

And yet, just one hour later, as they rounded the lighthouse, the wind died and the craft was becalmed. "Well, there's nothing to do but drop anchor," a cocky Pierre announced. "No telling how long we'll sit, but since the sun is shining for a change, I don't really care."

"How long before the wind usually picks up?" Jean asked, realizing how frantic his aunt and uncle would become if he failed to return before the drawbridge was drawn up.

"Well, let's just say no one should count on our services to-night," Pierre announced, his voice sounding lazier by the second. "You might as well lie back and enjoy our brief escape."

It was late afternoon when the wind picked up again, and the little boat began the arduous process of tacking back home.

"My father always said if I could navigate in this bay, I could sail just about anywhere," Pierre said as he deftly guided the shallop toward shore.

In the distance they could see the soldier's lantern flickering atop Dauphin Gate, and moments later the corps of drummers tapped *Le Retraite,* the signal that Louisbourg's gates were being closed.

"Well, Pierre," Jean said, "it looks like I'm stuck for the night."
Pierre shrugged his shoulders. "*C'est la vie,*" he answered.

Jean looked up at the starless sky and wondered how many more free nights would be in store for them. Despite all the uncertainty, he decided to enjoy himself and worry about Uncle Claude's wrath only when he had to face it the following day.

At breakfast the next morning, Monsieur André was uncharacteristically stern toward both boys.

"So I see you're back from your little escapade, aye?" he said in a sarcastic manner.

Pierre paused for a moment before answering. "Surely you're not upset about my going for a sail, Father. I finished my chores, and have been doing more than my share of work of late."

"That's precisely what I'm upset about. You've heard about the turn of events during these last few days, haven't you?"

"You mean the war, Father?"

"Indeed," he answered. "The sea is getting much too dangerous for joyrides. We sail now only for the fish. These times are too dangerous to risk losing boats and the people who sail them. No longer can you venture out alone and unarmed."

The gravity with which Monsieur André spoke startled Jean. It was only a few days back that war was announced, and overnight everyone had become so serious. With no enemy in sight and the security of living in a practically impregnable town, Jean couldn't help but feel that everyone was overreacting.

Jean excused himself at the sound of the morning drumroll. He ran all the way to town, stopping to collect himself before entering the *magasin*. Uncle Claude was opening the shutters and unlocking the windows—chores normally handled by Jean.

"Ah, Jean François!" Uncle Claude said, turning his massive body around in order to look squarely into Jean's eyes. "So, you've had a night on the town, I suppose, carrying on with those tavern wenches."

"Oh not at all, Uncle," he answered. "It's not like you think. I can explain."

"And what good will that do in the light of day after your poor aunt spent a sleepless night and I remain bitterly disappointed by your lack of responsibility?"

"But Uncle—" Jean tried to explain, only to be cut off.

"If you insist on associating with peasants then I might as well send you back to France where you'll have far more opportunity for such activity and where your family's reputation is not at stake."

Jean tried several more times to explain, but it became apparent that his uncle had already made up his mind and there was no changing him. Jean would simply have to take the verbal abuse, try to appear repentant, and hope that a customer would appear and bring a stop to this reprimanding.

But instead the two were interrupted by the shouts of angry men passing by the front door.

"We want food! We want food!" they chanted, wielding long sticks in the air. The group, made up mostly of fishermen, seemed to be heading for the King's Storehouse, where, it was common knowledge, there was always food and drink. Jean and his uncle followed behind but stopped short when a contingent of soldiers came running from several directions. They positioned themselves in front of the storehouse's massive doorway to form a human wall.

"Let us in!" the leader shouted. "Step aside and allow the food to be distributed to the workers."

"*Halte!*" the order came back. "Take one more step and we will fire."

The crowd of onlookers gasped and backed away as the protestors froze in position. Jean watched the soldiers cock their muskets and point bayonets directly at the motley gang. For a moment all was deadly quiet. And then the soldiers began marching forward, giving the protestors no option but to back away. As quickly as it began, the trouble was over.

What a sad moment for Louisbourg, Jean thought. For the first time, Frenchmen were fighting other Frenchmen over the most basic of human needs—food. Was this only a sample of what was to come, he wondered? If we can't take care of one another, can we ever get together enough to fight off an enemy?

"Come, Jean François, we can delay no longer. It is obvious now that we must take steps to make sure our little town survives."

Jean didn't quite understand what his uncle was talking about or why they were heading toward the home of Monsieur Lartigue, Louisbourg's wealthiest citizen.

Monsieur Lartigue met them at the front door and ushered them into a grand sitting room. Uncle Claude rushed through the amenities in order to get right down to business. Already aware of the gravity of Louisbourg's situation, Monsieur Lartigue was more than anxious to discuss solutions to their problems.

"I've come to enlist your aid to properly outfit my ships," Uncle Claude began.

"You're suggesting I get into privateering, are you?" Lartigue queried, knowing full well that the English merchant ships had been outfitted months ago and were already attacking French vessels at sea.

"I see no other way to ensure the safe arrival of our supplies," Uncle Claude replied. "If we don't arm our ships immediately I see no chance of Louisbourg surviving beyond six months."

"The storehouses are that low, *oui*?" Lartigue asked.

"Indeed. You realize, of course, that if you help us you receive twenty percent of the cargo's profit. I assure you this venture will be worth your while."

"*Oui*," Lartigue answered solemnly.

"It's not often that a man is able to make a profit while helping a cause at the same time," Uncle Claude said, trying further to persuade Lartigue.

The two continued talking about details for quite some time. Eventually Lartigue seemed satisfied with the deal, and the two Lelarges left feeling satisfied, too.

"Well, Jean," Uncle Claude said as the two ambled home, "we have a chance now, to survive this trouble we find ourselves in. Let us hope and pray, my boy, that there is a happy ending."

Jean François Lelarge and Pierre André spent many hours during the next few months strolling about the moors beyond the fortress walls, contemplating what was to become of their town, their families, and their lives. French raids on English ships went very well in the early part of the summer. However, the tide turned in August and the ships of Louisbourg faced many losses. As English prisoners filled the jails of the tiny town and further taxed the food supplies, a quiet desperation overtook the once peaceful settlement. The young men were forced to take up muskets and train with the militia. Horror stories of captured ships and enemy blockades weakened the prospects for a happy ending.

After a year of hardship the town was captured by an army of New Englanders backed by the British navy, and most citizens were sent back to France. Pierre's life would be that of a Brittany fisherman—not much different from his life in Louisbourg. Jean, however, having no family left in France, boarded one of his uncle's merchant ships in November, before the shipping lanes closed, and eventually settled in Louisiana, which was a more established French settlement in the New World.

Acknowledgments

We are most grateful for the tremendous hospitality offered to us by the Canadian Park Service, the employees of the Fortress of Louisbourg, and particularly the costumed interpreters who co-operated scene by scene and deftly reenacted our story. We also extend deep gratitude to our leading men, Chad Magee and Marc LeBlanc, as well as to Peter Chiasson and his lovely wife, Sandy, for their on- and off-camera work.

Because this is a seafaring story we could not have survived without Brian Harpell's knowledge of the fishing industry, his ability to sail antique boats, and his constant guidance in determining the historical accuracy of each scene. John Johnston and Terry McCalmont, both on-site historians, helped us understand the French perspective and reviewed outlines and drafts of the book. We thank Gordon Maclean of the Park Service, who captained his power boat for hours in cold, foggy waters until we got just the right shot of the city. And, finally, thanks to Ann O'Neill for several conferences and the scheduling of interpreters. *Merci!*

JOAN ANDERSON
GEORGE ANCONA

About the Author and Photographer

JOAN ANDERSON and GEORGE ANCONA have worked together on many award-winning books. Author Joan Anderson says: "Having done books on all the other early European settlers of the New World, I wanted to complete the study by focusing on the French. I marvel at the flourish with which they settled the New World."

Photographer George Ancona says: "It all started with Cajun cuisine and music. I began to inquire about the history of the Cajun people in Louisiana, and that brought me back to Nova Scotia. I've always been curious about where people come from, their food, music, and dancing."

Joan Anderson lives in Pearl River, New York. George Ancona lives in Stony Point, New York.